doll School

Design a Day of Learning and Play!

★ American Girl®

Published by American Girl Publishing
Copyright © 2016 American Girl

Questions or comments? Call 1-800-845-0005,
visit americangirl.com, or write to Customer Service,
American Girl, 8400 Fairway Place, Middleton, WI 53562-0497.

Printed in China
16 17 18 19 20 21 LEO 10 9 8 7 6 5 4 3

Editorial Development: Emily Osborn
Art Direction and Design: Jessica Annoye
Production: Jeannette Bailey, Laura Markowitz, Cynthia Stiles, Kristi Tabrizi
Photography: Joe Hinirichs, Youa Thao, Derek Brabender
Craft Styling: Emily Osborn, Melissa Seymour
Set Styling: Casey Hull, Kim Sphar, Emma Wimberley
Doll Styling: Karen Timm, Meghan Hurley
Illustrations: Monika Roe

Dear Reader,

Do you enjoy going to school? What's your favorite subject? Math? Art? Science? Do you have a special hangout, like the library, playground, or cafeteria? There are all kinds of fun things that can happen when you're at school—journaling during English, making an aquarium in Science, scoring a goal in Gym, or learning about new countries in Geography.

This book will help you create a school of your very own for you and your doll. Use the kit's flash cards to study for a math quiz, the composition book to write down her thoughts, and the world map to mark where she'd like to visit. Create instruments for her to play during Music, or books to read when in the library, and make her very own locker to store all of her school keepsakes.

There's the bell!

Your friends at American Girl

Craft with Care

Keep Your Doll Safe

When creating doll crafts, remember that dyes from ribbons, felt, beads, cords, fabrics, fleece, and other supplies may bleed onto your doll and pet or their clothes and leave permanent stains. To help prevent this, use lighter colors when possible, and check your doll and her pet often to make sure the colors aren't transferring to their bodies, vinyl, or clothes or to the pet's fur. And never get your doll or pet wet! Water and heat greatly increase dye rub-off.

Get Help!

When you see this symbol 🖐 in the book, it means that you need an adult to help you with all or a part of the craft. ALWAYS ask for help before continuing.

Ask First

If a craft asks you to use any old item, such as a shirt or sock, always ask an adult for permission before you use it. Your parent might still need it, so check first.

Craft Smart

If a craft instruction says "cut," use scissors. If it says "glue," use craft glue or adhesive dots. And if it says "paint," use a nontoxic acrylic paint. Before you use these supplies, ask an adult to check them over—especially paints and glues. Some crafting supplies are not safe for kids.

Put Up Crafts and Supplies

When you're not using the crafts or art supplies, put them up high or store them away from little kids and pets. Toddlers and animals might eat your crafts, break them, or even hurt themselves when playing with them.

WARNING

Safely tuck your doll and her pets away while you craft so that paint, glue, and other messy supplies don't get on them. Make sure each craft project dries completely before you let your doll or her pet near it.

Locker

Store all of your doll's school supplies in here.

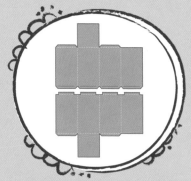

1. Lay the two halves of the locker flat. The half with slots should go above the half with tabs. Line up the 4 tabs with the 4 slots.

2. Insert the tabs into the slots and tape to secure. Stand the locker up and form into a tall rectangular box.

3. Fold the top of the locker down and tape it to the tabs on the sides to secure. Repeat for bottom of locker.

4. Insert the locker shelf by taping the tabs into the inside of the locker. Use the mirror sticker, and punch out friends' photos from the kit to decorate the inside of the locker door.

Before Class

Make these crafts so your doll has a place for all of her things to get her through the day.

Backpack

Every girl going to school needs a nice backpack to carry her books. Cut two pieces of ribbon that are 9 inches long for the straps. Glue plastic clips to one end of each ribbon. Once dry, glue the plastic clipped ends of the ribbons to the bottom back of a drawstring bag roughly 7 inches in size. Let dry. Glue the other ends of the ribbons to the top back of the bag. Cut out a 3-by-3-inch piece of self-sticking felt and place it on the bottom half of the backpack to look like a pocket. Cut out a 2-by-3-inch piece of self-sticking felt and glue to the top half of the backpack to look like a small pocket. Remove the drawstring from the bag. Glue the bag opening closed. Let dry. Glue a 9-inch-long zipper across the top. Allow time to dry. Use washi tape to decorate the backpack pockets. Your doll is ready to go to school in style.

Science

Your doll will see a special view of nature during Science class!

Aquarium

Use a 4-inch plastic cube for an aquarium. Cut a piece of textured blue paper into a 4-inch-by-4-inch square. Glue it to the inside of the cube. Put fish stickers onto the blue paper. Use adhesive dots to stick paper greenery and ocean stickers to the inside front of the cube. Display in your doll's Science class.

Microscope

Paint a 4-inch watch stand a bright color using nontoxic metallic acrylic paint. Let dry. Glue a marker cap to the underside of the curve. Paint a ½-by-1-inch wooden rectangle and two small wooden wheels black. Once dry, glue the rectangle piece to the top of the curve, then the two wheels to the rectangle piece. Glue two smaller marker caps upside-down to the wheels. Let dry. For the specimen slide, cut out a 1½-by-1½-inch square of paper and glue two small silver barrette clips to the center. Use vellum paper or plastic sheets for slides.

Periodic Table

Use the kit's periodic table and hang it on your doll's wall so she can learn all the elements!

Tabletop Easel
Make a stand for your works of art!

1. Glue two craft sticks into the shape of an upside-down V.

2. Once that is dry, place glue along the edge of a third craft stick.

3. Attach the third stick across the first two.

4. For the stand, attach one end of a craft stick to the point using poster putty. This will allow some flexibility to balance your artwork. Create your doll's very own masterpiece by painting on the canvas included in the kit.

Art Class

Your creativity will soar with these art assignments.

Paintbrushes

Ask an adult to cut a cake-pop stick in half. Paint the small stick a bright color using nontoxic acrylic paint. Let dry. Cut a small section of bristles from an old paintbrush. Glue the bristles to one end of the cake-pop stick. Let dry. Cut a tiny rectangle of silver duct tape and wrap it around the base of the bristles.

Crayons

Ask an adult to help you cut 5 toothpicks in half. Paint or use a marker to color each toothpick a different shade. Punch out and construct the crayon box from the kit. Once dry, place the crayons inside the box, point side up.

Watercolor Palette

Cut out a ½-by-2-inch piece of cardboard. Paint it white. Let dry. Paint 6 dots (red, orange, yellow, green, blue, and purple) in a row along one side of the cardboard. Ask an adult to cut a plastic toothpick in half. Cut a small section of bristles from an old paintbrush. Glue the bristles to the cut end of the toothpick. Let dry. Cut a tiny rectangle of silver duct tape and wrap it around the base of the bristles. Glue the paintbrush onto the cardboard alongside the paint pods. Ask an adult to help cut a ½-by-2-inch piece of plastic. Glue the plastic on top of the palette. Let dry.

Picture Day

Help your doll remember this best school year ever with a picture.

Photo Tip Sheet

School photos are important keepsakes, so make sure your doll looks her best on picture day. Review the tip sheet from the kit with your doll the day before the photo shoot so she is prepared.

Photo Backgrounds

Nothing says "school photo" like traditional streaky backgrounds. To make them, use watercolor paint on white construction or drawing paper.

Photo Studio

Paint a small wooden crate and a mini clipboard white. Let dry. Glue the bottom edge of the clipboard to a short edge on the bottom of the crate. Once dry, stand the crate on its side so the clipboard is upright. Clip one of your photo backgrounds to the clipboard. Your doll is now ready for her picture!

School Photos

Students love sharing school photos. Pull out the school photos and pass them around.

Recess

Now is the time to recharge between classes.

Swing Set

Paint five 14-inch papiér-mâché craft letters white—one capital I, one T, one V, and two A's. Let dry. Glue the I and T together. This will be the top bar of the swing set. Then glue the two A's on each end of the top bar. Glue the V upside-down in the middle. Let dry. Cut out two 3-by- 1 ½-inch pieces of craft foam for swing seats. Using a standard hole punch, punch one hole on each end of the foam. Cut four 11-inch pieces of jute rope or thick yarn. Dip the ends of your rope in craft glue so they don't fray. Once the ends are dry, thread one end of each rope through a hole and knot it securely in place. Tie the rope around the top bar, one swing on each side of the upside-down V.

Hula Hoop

Use the inside circle from a plastic embroidery hoop to make this craft, and see how long your doll can hula hoop until the circle drops.

Kickball

Enjoy a riveting game of kickball. Paint a 3-inch-diameter papiér-mâché ball the bright color of your choice. Let dry. Now your doll is ready to play!

Lunch

Students line up for a trip to the cafeteria to get some lunch.

Food Tray

Lay a sheet of paper on a small rectangular plastic lid for a tray. Cut or punch out a craft foam circle for a plate. Help your doll hold her tray by wrapping a clear elastic band around her wrists to bring her hands closer together.

Food

For pretend sandwich bread, ask an adult to help you cut small triangles from white foam core or small squares out of corkboard, and color in the edges with brown marker for crust. Punch out fun shapes from colored paper for fillings. For an apple, ask an adult to cut the ends off a toothpick. Color the toothpick with a brown marker; then punch out a leaf shape from green paper. Glue them inside a red bead. Use the kit's menu to feature today's lunch specials.

Lunch Counter

Stack and glue or tape together three 3 ¾-by-9 ½-by-4-inch cupcake boxes with windows. Use washi tape to cover up the seams. Place cupcake holder in the top cupcake box. Glue fake food into silver cupcake liners and place them inside the holder in the top box.

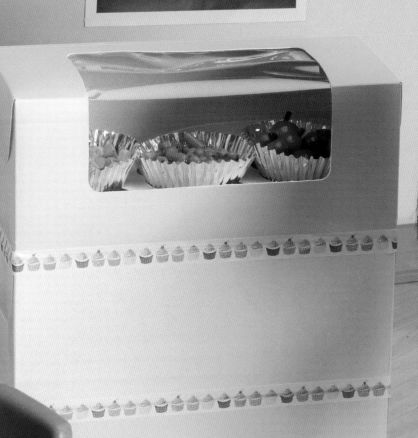

Today's Specials

- Macaroni with Cheese $2.50
- Peas and Carrots $.75
- Veggie Sandwich $3.00
- Apple $.50

Language Arts

Your doll will love to learn how to read and write in this class.

Composition Notebook

Punch out the composition notebook cover included in the kit. Cut out pieces of lined paper to fit inside the cover, about 2 ¾ inches long by 2 inches wide. Staple the lined pages together along a long edge. To attach the composition cover, place glue on the front of the first lined page and the back of the last lined page and wrap the cover around them, smoothing it by pressing down with your fingers.

Pencil

Make a pencil for your doll, so she can write in her composition book. Ask an adult to cut a toothpick in half. Then, using a pink marker, color in the tip of the flat end for the eraser. Color the body of the toothpick with a yellow marker, stopping a tiny bit above the tip, so it looks like the pencil was sharpened. Then take a black marker and color in the pointed tip for the graphite. Finally, cut a tiny piece of silver duct tape and wrap it around the toothpick just below the pink eraser.

Music Room

A chance to play an instrument is music to your doll's ears.

Clarinet

Make this reed instrument with a 5-inch bamboo lollipop stick. Paint or use a marker to color the stick black, except for one side of the pointed end. The wood-colored part will act as the clarinet reed. Set aside. Paint a flat-end toothpick and 11 seed beads silver. Let dry. Ask an adult to help cut the toothpick in half and glue it to the dowel. Glue seed beads next to the toothpick halves for keys. Cut out two half-circles from black felt and glue to the bottom of the clarinet for the bell. Once dry, use silver paint or a silver marker to draw lines around the clarinet to show the clarinet joints. Help your doll hold the clarinet by wrapping a clear elastic band around her wrists to bring her hands closer together.

Electric Keyboard

Use double-sided tape to attach glittery paper to the outside of a shoebox lid. Punch out the keyboard from the kit and tape it to the lid. For each leg, tape hard-candy rolls together end to end. Wrap the rolls in plain paper, and tape them closed. Wrap a third roll in plain paper and glue it in between the legs to help them balance. Once dry, balance the piano over the legs.

Flute

Your doll might get into treble with this instrument.

1. Glue seed beads to a small straw.

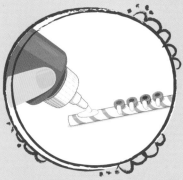

2. Use tacky glue to "draw" lines over and next to the beads to create keys and to "draw" an oval near one end for a mouthpiece. Let dry.

3. Paint the entire instrument silver, including inside the beads. Let dry.

4. Use a black marker to draw a dot on the mouthpiece for the hole.

FINISH!

Field Day

Your doll will have a blast participating in these outdoor races.

Potato Sack Race
Use jute or burlap bags as potato sacks for each doll. Now your dolls are ready to hop toward the finish line!

Three-Legged Race
Use ribbon hair ties to secure one doll's right leg to another doll's left leg. The dolls need to work together to win this event without falling down!

Mile Run
This race is the main event during Field Day. Everyone runs a mile to cap off a fun day filled with sports. And, of course, every race needs a finish line. Use the "Finish!" banner from the kit to mark the end of the route.

Tug-of-War
Use an 11-inch rope dog toy for your doll and a friend to play this classic game. Help your doll hold the rope by wrapping a clear elastic band around her wrist and the rope.

Field Day Tees
Help your doll look the part by punching out a Field Day logo and taping it to one of her shirts.

Library

Learn about the magic and information that come from books.

Bookshelves

Create a place for the school's library books. Take the bottom half of a bead/craft organizer and glue a piece of brown construction paper to its back. Glue a piece of cardboard to one of the box's longer edges to help the box stand on its side. Let dry.

Books

Give your doll plenty to read by stocking the school library with books. Punch out the book covers in the kit or miniaturize your favorite books to create a fun book collection for your doll. To make your own, lay the front and back covers flat on a printer and reduce them to 33 percent. Cut out each cover, and glue a piece of cardboard or folded paper along the inside. Place inside the bookcase.

Library Cards

Each student accesses the library with her own library card. Pull out the card from the kit and fill in your doll's name. If you have more than one doll, photocopy the card before you fill it out.

Due Date Stamp

Make sure students return their books on time with this due date stamp.

1. ✋ Ask an adult to help cut six 1-by-1-inch pieces of cardboard.

2. Glue the cardboard pieces together; then paint them silver. Let dry.

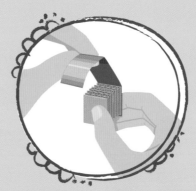

3. Cut out a 3-by-1-inch piece of silver duct tape and wrap it around 3 sides of the cardboard.

4. Glue a mini wooden drawer pull on top. Let dry. Punch out the checkout cards from the kit to stamp the due date as your doll checks out some books!

WORLD MAP

ARCTIC OCEAN

NORTH
AMERICA

ATLANTIC
OCEAN

EUROPE

ASIA

PACIFIC
OCEAN

AFRICA

PACIFIC
OCEAN

SOUTH
AMERICA

INDIAN
OCEAN

AUSTRALIA

ATLANTIC
OCEAN

ANTARCTICA

Geography

Help your doll learn about the world she lives in.

World Map

The world is a big and exciting place filled with continents and oceans. Pull out the kit's map. Have your doll place star stickers to mark places she would like to visit.

27

Computer Room

Put your doll's typing and Internet-searching skills to the test with her very own desktop computer.

Computer and Keyboard

Ask an adult to cut a slit in the bottom of a miniature paper cup. Glue a small craft stick into the slit. Cut a 3 ½-by-2 ¾-inch piece of craft foam for the monitor. Use the computer sticker from the kit for the screen. Glue or tape the monitor to the craft stick. Cut out a ½-by-3 ½-inch piece of craft foam for the keyboard. Place the kit's keyboard sticker onto the craft foam. Glue a ¼-by-3 ½-inch strip of craft foam to the top edge of the keyboard to help prop it up.

Mouse

Use a large oval craft jewel for the mouse. Glue one end of a 4-inch piece of thread to the bottom of the jewel. Tape the other end of the thread to the monitor's miniature cup. Cut out a 1-by-1 ¼-inch piece of paper for a mouse pad. Your doll is now ready to surf the Web.